Dear Parent:
Your child's love of reading starts here!

Every child learns to read in a different way and at his or her own speed. Some go back and forth between reading levels and read favorite books again and again. Others read through each level in order. You can help your young reader improve and become more confident by encouraging his or her own interests and abilities. From books your child reads with you to the first books he or she reads alone, there are I Can Read Books for every stage of reading:

SHARED READING
Basic language, word repetition, and whimsical illustrations, ideal for sharing with your emergent reader

BEGINNING READING
Short sentences, familiar words, and simple concepts for children eager to read on their

READING WITH HELP
Engaging stories, longer sentences, ; for developing readers

READING ALONE
Complex plots, challenging vocabulary, and high-interest topics for the independent reader

I Can Read Books have introduced children to the joy of reading since 1957. Featuring award-winning authors and illustrators and a fabulous cast of beloved characters, I Can Read Books set the standard for beginning readers.

A lifetime of discovery begins with the magical words "I Can Read!"

Visit www.icanread.com for information
on enriching your child's reading experience.

Visit www.zonderkidz.com/icanread for more faith-based
I Can Read! titles from Zonderkidz.

And now, do not be distressed and do not be
angry with yourselves for selling me here, because it
was to save lives that God sent me ahead of you.
—Genesis 45:5

ZONDERKIDZ

Joseph the Dreamer
Copyright © 2015 by Zondervan
Illustrations © 2015 by David Miles

An **I Can Read Book**

Requests for information should be addressed to:
Zonderkidz, 3900 Sparks Drive SE, Grand Rapids, Michigan 49546

ISBN 978-0-310-75084-0

Editor: Mary Hassinger
Art direction: Deborah Washburn

ZONDER**kidz**

Reading 2 with help

I Can Read!

Joseph the Dreamer

Pictures by David Miles

ZONDER**kidz**
.com

Joseph had a lot of brothers.

Joseph was young.

And he was his father's favorite.

One day, Joseph's father gave him a robe.

It had many colors.

Joseph loved it!

When Joseph's brothers saw his robe,

they were jealous.

They asked, "Why don't we get new robes?

What makes Joseph so special?"

Then Joseph had a dream.

He told his brothers,

"Last night,

I dreamed we were picking grain.

Your bunches of grain

all bowed down to mine."

Joseph's brothers were upset.

They asked,

"Does he think he is better than us?

Does he think we should bow to him?"

They made a plan to get rid of Joseph.

One day, Joseph was out in a field.

His brothers grabbed him.

They threw him in an empty well.

Joseph was scared.
He didn't understand
why his brothers hated him,
and the well was dark.

Then someone threw down a rope.

They pulled Joseph out.

Joseph's brothers told him,

"We're selling you as a slave."

Joseph's brothers dipped his colorful robe in goat's blood. They showed their father. They said, "Your son has been killed by a wild animal."

Joseph's father was very, very sad.

Joseph traveled with the slave traders.

They went all the way to Egypt.

In Egypt, Joseph was sold

to a rich man.

The rich man threw Joseph in jail.

Joseph hadn't even done anything wrong!

But God was with Joseph.

In jail, Joseph met a man

who used to be the king's servant.

The servant had a dream.

He said to Joseph,

"I dreamed I made a drink from grapes.

Then I gave the drink to the king.

Can you tell me what this means?"

Joseph said,

"God knows about your dream.

It means that soon

you will work for the king again."

Joseph was right.

A few days later,

the servant got out of jail.

"Don't forget about me,"

Joseph said to him.

Later, the king had a dream.

No one could tell him what it meant.

But the king's servant remembered.

"Joseph can tell you

what your dream means!" he said.

The king sent for Joseph.

He told Joseph his dream.

Joseph said,

"Lots of food will grow for seven years.

Then the food will stop growing.

God wants us to save food now,

so we won't be hungry later."

The king was impressed.
He put Joseph in charge
of all the food in Egypt.

Everything Joseph said came true.

For seven years lots of food grew.

Then the seven bad years began.

Even Joseph's family did not have

enough to eat.

Joseph's father sent his sons

to buy food in Egypt.

When Joseph's brothers arrived,
they bowed to Joseph.
It was just like Joseph's dream.
But they did not know
he was their brother.
Joseph knew.

Joseph sold his brothers food,

and they went home.

Later, the brothers came back
to buy more food.

They bowed to Joseph again.

This time Joseph said,

"Don't you recognize me?

I'm your brother, Joseph!"

His brothers were afraid.
Would Joseph hate them
for what they had done?

29

But Joseph said,

"I forgive you.

What you did to me was bad,

but God used it for good."

They all hugged.

The brothers rushed home.

They told their father,

"Joseph is alive!"

Soon the whole family moved to Egypt.

People of the Bible

Your father's God helps you.
He gives you blessings from the highest heaven.
— *Genesis 49:25*

Jacob

Jacob was one of Isaac's sons. He cheated his twin brother Esau out of his inheritance from their father. Jacob left home to escape his angry brother. But God promised Jacob he would watch over him wherever he went. And he was blessed with twelve sons.

Joseph

Joseph was the son of Jacob and Rachel. He was Jacob's favorite son and was treated the best. His brothers were jealous and sold him as a slave, but God used that bad thing for good. He knew that he would use Joseph to help save many people during a famine.

Life in Bible Times
Joseph's Colorful Coat

Jacob gave his favorite son, Joseph, a beautiful coat that was made with very colorful threads. Clothing like this was usually meant for special people and events. Since only Joseph got a coat like this from their father, his brothers knew he was Jacob's favorite.

www.ingramcontent.com/pod-product-compliance
Ingram Content Group UK Ltd.
Pitfield, Milton Keynes, MK11 3LW, UK
UKHW020024180625
459797UK00001B/9

Dear Parent:
Your child's love of reading starts here!

Every child learns to read in a different way and at his or her own speed. Some go back and forth between reading levels and read favorite books again and again. Others read through each level in order. You can help your young reader improve and become more confident by encouraging his or her own interests and abilities. From books your child reads with you to the first books he or she reads alone, there are I Can Read Books for every stage of reading:

SHARED READING
Basic language, word repetition, and whimsical illustrations ideal for sharing with your emergent reader

BEGINNING READING
Short sentences, familiar words, and simple concepts for children eager to read on their own

READING WITH HELP
Engaging stories, longer sentences, and language play for developing readers

READING ALONE
Complex plots, challenging vocabulary, and high-interest topics for the independent reader

I Can Read Books have introduced children to the joy of reading since 1957. Featuring award-winning authors and illustrators and a fabulous cast of beloved characters, I Can Read Books set the standard for beginning readers.

A lifetime of discovery begins with the magical words "I Can Read!"

Visit www.icanread.com for information
on enriching your child's reading experience.

Visit www.zonderkidz.com/icanread for more faith-based
I Can Read! titles from Zonderkidz.

" 'I will take you to be my own people. I will
be your God. You will know that I am the
Lord your God when I throw off the load the
Egyptians have put on your shoulders.' "
—*Exodus 6:7*

ZONDERKIDZ

Moses and the King
Copyright © 2009 by Mission City Press. All Rights Reserved.
All Beginner's Bible copyrights and trademarks (including art, text, characters, etc.)
are owned by Mission City Press and licensed by Zondervan of Grand Rapids,
Michigan.

An **I Can Read Book**

Requests for information should be addressed to:
Zonderkidz, 3900 *Sparks Drive SE, Grand Rapids, Michigan* 49546

Library of Congress Cataloging-in-Publication Data

Pulley, Kelly.
    Moses and the King / illustrated by Kelly Pulley.
        p. cm. -- (I can read levels)
        ISBN 978-0-310-71800-0 (softcover)
        1. Moses (Biblical leader)--Juvenile literature. 2. Exodus, The--Juvenile
        literature. 3. Bible stories, English--O.T. Exodus. I. Title.
    BS580.M6P85 2009
    222'.1209505--dc22
                              2008038635

All Scripture quotations unless otherwise noted are taken from The Holy Bible,
New International Reader's Version®, NIrV®. Copyright © 1995, 1996, 1998 by Biblica,
Inc.® Used by permission. All rights reserved worldwide.

Any internet addresses (websites, blogs, etc.) and telephone numbers printed in this
book are offered as a resource. They are not intended in any way to be or imply an
endorsement by Zondervan, nor does Zondervan vouch for the content of these sites
and numbers for the life of this book.

No part of this publication may be reproduced, stored in a retrieval system, or
transmitted in any form or by any means—electronic, mechanical, photocopy,
recording, or any other—except for brief quotations in printed reviews, without the
prior permission of the publisher.

Zonderkidz is a trademark of Zondervan.

I Can Read® and I Can Read Book® are trademarks of HarperCollins Publishers.

Art Direction & Design: Jody Langley

Moses and the King

Pictures by Kelly Pulley
and Paul Trice

God's people were slaves.

A mean king ruled the slaves.

Moses was scared
of the mean king.
So Moses ran away.

God wanted Moses

to help the slaves.

Moses did not know how.

8

One day, God spoke to Moses
from a burning bush.
"Moses, go back
and save my people.
Take them to a new land."

Moses was afraid.

"The king will not listen to me,"

said Moses.

"I will help you talk
to the king," God said.

Moses went to see the king.

"Let God's people go,"
Moses said to the king.

The king said,
"No! The slaves cannot go.
I do not know your God."

"My God is powerful.
You will see what my God
can do," said Moses.

God changed the river water.
Nobody could drink it.

The king said, "No!
The slaves cannot go."

God sent frogs.

God sent
bugs.

God sent
sickness.

Still the king said,

"No, no, no."

God made the sky dark.

Still the king said,

"No! The slaves cannot go."

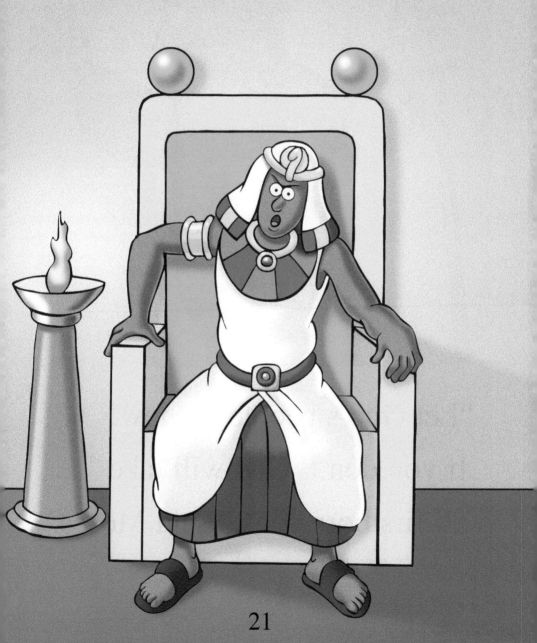

"Let God's people go now!
If you don't, God will take
all firstborn sons," said Moses.

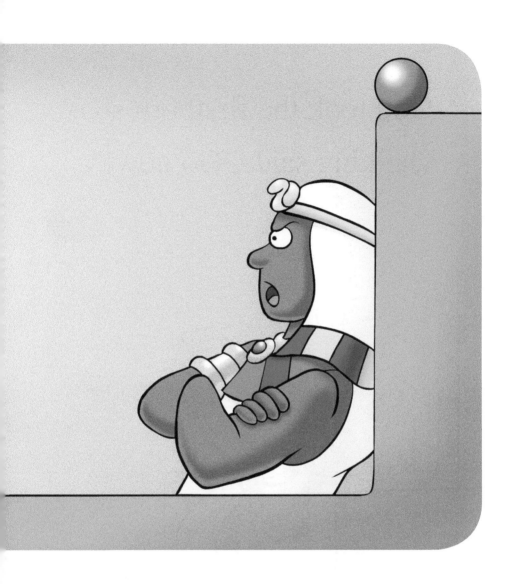

"No! The slaves cannot go,"
said the mean king.

God took the firstborn sons.

The king said, "Go now!"

So Moses led the people
out of the city.
They went to the Red Sea.

The king and his army chased
Moses and God's people.

"We are trapped by the sea!
What do we do now?"
the people asked.

God sent a big cloud.
The king and his army
could not see.

God said to Moses,
"Reach your hand over the sea."

God parted the water.

Moses and the people ran

to the other side.

The king and his army
were close behind.

God made the water crash down
on the king's army.
Moses and the slaves were free!

www.ingramcontent.com/pod-product-compliance
Ingram Content Group UK Ltd.
Pitfield, Milton Keynes, MK11 3LW, UK
UKHW020024180625
459797UK00001B/5